The Route

and Other Poems

The Route
and Other Poems

by

James R. Scrimgeour

To Doris

All Best,

Enjoy!

[illegible signature]

The PIKESTAFF PRESS

ISBN: 0-936044-07-1

Library of Congress Catalog Card Number: 96-68654

The PIKESTAFF PRESS
P.O. Box 127
Normal, Illinois 61761

Printed in the United States of America

This book is dedicated to Christine Xanthakos Scrimgeour and Aidan FitzGerald Scrimgeour for all the joy they have given and all they will give.

Contents

The Faces

that come to me in the night,
in the last minutes before sleep,
faces rolling in and out
of the fog banks over the black-red sea
on the backs of my eyelids —

Blake called them angels,
                                        but for me
they are ancestors, human beings
who share my genes, humans
in direct lines, ghostly figures
becoming clear, distinct,
                                        look there, my father,
his sorrowful, drawn smile and my mother,
her fierce strength, not yet blank, nor resigned,
and so many others flitting in and out of vision —

                                        that one there
with the gray hair — Mary Towne Estey, perhaps,
under blue Salem skies riding on the cart
to the top of the hill . . . pleading
"lest other innocent blood be shed" . . .

or is it my grandmother, Mattie Cummings, as serene,
as calm, riding cross country through Minneapolis
and on to San Francisco in her private railroad coach
after her daughters, her brother, and her husband died . . .

Or that one — perhaps — the Reverend James —
righteous and stern — in his Newburgh pulpit —
high on his snuff . . .
                                        the faces coming into focus,
so clear, the lines of wisdom, of fear,
of care, for split seconds before fading
into air . . .
                              Blake took dictation, but for me —
no angels, just faces — no words —
just brief encounters — human contact
with clear deep, deep, imploring eyes.

imploring me for words — their words
I will have to find — in old books,
on old Indian trails, winding along
the banks of river,
                                        and in the deep recesses,
the older, darker trails in my own mind.

The Route

— After Mary Towne Estey (1634 - 1692) —

Witchcraft was hung in History,
But History and I
Find all the Witchcraft that we need
Around us, every day —

— Emily Dickinson

I

Start at the Sheriff's office on St. Peter's Street,
at the red brick box building — go past the vacant lot
with strewn rubbish and the chain link fence,
go straight until you run smack into the five story
parking garage.
                                        Detour round the imposing structure,
enter the East India Square Mall, complete
with:
                           health food restaurants (self-serve yogurt,
fruit juice, etc),
                                        the visitor's center
with all the maps you'll ever need,

a movie theater with three featured attractions:
("Free Willy," "Much Ado about Nothing," and
"Silk Stalkings"),
                                                  and a real life stalker,
an overweight male with stubble beard and dangling
dirty T shirt, lounging against a cream column.

Exit through the revolving glass doors.

Note the fountain with water pouring
through the notches in the square teeth
sticking up out of a cement jaw lying comfortably
on top of the two round stone pillars —
                                                            square teeth — fixed
in a cement Cheshire Cat smile —

the water falling about 15 ft into the pool —
children laughing, leapfrogging
on stone lily pads —

II

Turn right onto
Essex street — red brick cobblestone —
complete with shops, shops, and more shops —
"The Dancer's Partner," "Jack's Ladies Apparel,"
"Custom House Gallery," and the "Derby Street
Book Store" with *Great Lives of the Twentieth
Century* prominently featured in the window.

Check out the displays, the fliers —
the U.S. Army recruitment station — the office
of Salem State Downtown College,

pass by the smiling blonde asking,
"Am I funny?" the man with her — silent,
stroking her bare shoulder,
the people
in 17th century costumes handing out fliers
on "Cry Innocent" — a skit
after which the audience votes, decides
the fate of Bridget Bishop,
and the man
with the brochures for "Dracula's Castle"
("Salem's Haunted House" — "fun for everyone")
the man in the Vampire suit muttering,
"It's hot! God, it's hot."

examine strictly these afflicted persons
and keep them apart for some time,

III

browse through the trinkets on sidewalk tables —
the witch mugs, witch buttons, witch postcards,
witch bells, and

(take a parenthesis
to tell the shopkeeper who asks belligerently,
"What are you writing in that notebook?"

that you're keeping a journal, a record
of the journey as you retrace the route my great,
great, great, great, great, great,
great grandmother took (with seven others)
on the back of a jouncing cart as it lurched
from the jail (for the fourth and last time)
to Gallows Hill on September 22, 1692,
that you're interested in the contrasting view —

"Why don't you put in the witch pennies
while you're at it?" he asks)

witch pennies — three for a dollar,

through the "Witch City" T shirts, "Salem,
a Bewitchingly Good Time," reads one.

(neglect to mention Thomas Perkins, juror,
who sat in judgment of the accused witches,
Thomas Perkins (1659 - 1722), whose blood
is also coursing in my veins)

IV

rest on the stone bench at the busy intersection
of Essex and Washington, watch the water
of this second fountain pour out of the five holes
in the large rectangular stone slab —

(and think of the sign right there in the window
of "The Zodiac Room" which features Salem witches,
psychic readings, magical gifts, and Diana,
an internationally known psychic who has clients
in all parts of the U.S. and Canada, who has worked
with police in the investigations of murders,
and who employs "Psychometry," "tone vibrations,"
and "past life regression," Diana, who does the utmost
in her powers of discovery and detection)

— the stone slab, a large gravestone
with ghostly figures carved in it —

the water streaming forth like five men urinating —
look that one there, that puny stream, the oldest —
needs prostate surgery.

V

Get up, start again, cross Washington,
note the quaint red cobblestones in the street
have turned to plain asphalt, see Essex divided

this side — suburban — a neat
mini-park with benches,
young trees
with small protective fences and piles
of wood chips at the base, planted
in the middle of the sidewalk,
and the Essex House
with one and two bedroom apartments
now renting —

while on the other,
the far side, the "Witch House" (actually
the restored home of Judge Corwin), and

the sign with the arrow pointing up the alley
to the

Witch Dungeon Museum

which gives one ample time to browse
in the gift shop before the show, before
entering the hall with 21 plaques
on the wall,
time to read each plaque,
each anecdote, each snap shot, hung
on the periphery — including
one on Tabitha and the girls,
one on John Willard, the constable
who didn't believe them, — and one
on the Reverend Samuel Paris who did,

surrounded by anecdotes of the poison
before the carefully rehearsed introduction,
the dramatic reenactment,
the encounter
between an accused witch and Ann Putnam,
one of her accusers,
well done foreplay
before being led down in darkness, led down
the winding stairs to the dungeons,
to the dark cells carefully created to match
the remains discovered in the excavation —

the larger cells
(6-8' square) for the accused who could afford
to pay for their chains and lodgings,

in each cell a wax woman
in varying stages of distress,

the cells
turning into smaller and smaller
and smaller cells where poor women died
saving the expense and bother of a trial . . .

the way turning darker, the shadows
still blacker, the cells still smaller until
in one of the last showrooms, the replica
of the poorest woman, hunched, standing
in a cubicle the size of a telephone booth
without a change of clothes —

and suddenly — the cheap trick —

the wax figure
moves, a live woman's hands stretch, reach out
across the centuries to us —

our screams!

VI

. . . echoes in the void . . . floating . . .

aside . . .

the bill of Robert Lord,
blacksmith, who lived and plied his trade
on the site of the Samuel Baker house on High St.
the bill presented in July 1692:

Item: "for making fouer payer
of Iron ffetters and tow payer of hand Cuffs
and putting them on to ye legs and hands
of Goodwife Cloys, Bromidg, Green, and Estes
all att one pound aleven Shillings money L S D
1-11-0"

and landing next to
— Isaiah Stone's souvenir and gift shop
with a large witch on the sidewalk in front,
the witch — his second —
he wheels out
every day to the curb —

this witch (he sold his first)
with straw broom, pointy black hat,
long black dress, (which covers her old wire
laundry basket body)
complete with
ash grey mask face, bright blood red lips
and mirrors in the eye slots —

"eyes are the mirror
of the soul," Isaiah says, seriously,

listen to this prophet, who tells tourists
"there are no witches in Salem," yet stocks
his store with the same trinkets —
this same Isaiah
who says simply, "I'd sell pornography . . .
If people will buy, I'll sell! . . .
this witch —
I'll let it go for $300.00."

VII

pause for a moment, let it all sink in

before the first church in Salem — Unitarian,
gathered "in the liberal Christian tradition,"
in 1629 (which is, I believe, 92 backwards)

read the commemorative plaque: "We covenant
with the Lord and one with another, and do bind
ourselves in the presence of God to walk together
in all his ways, according as he is pleased
to reveal himself unto us in his blessed word
of truth."

go past the Ropes mansion . . . greet the young male
on his knees on the red brick sidewalk weeding out
the grass in the cracks —

                                        his clear section,

in front of his house,

                                        stands out,

VIII

walk through this middle class
residential neighborhood, check out
the old New England houses on both sides

pause, press your face to the wrought iron bars,
look through the black sharp pike fence, at the dry
black fountain on the dry brown lawn, look through
at the Salem Public Library, at yet another
red brick building
                    (red brick —
a modern Salem motif)
                    listen to the hubbub —
the confused tourist holding up traffic,
the herd, the horns blaring, the word
"asshole," floating in the air

think of all the innocent blood that will be shed
which cannot be avoided in the way and course we go,

sweat profusely in the heat, pick up the pace,
pass quickly by the Grace Episcopal Church,
the Quaker meeting house, and the shingle,
"Steven B. Hayes, Psychiatrist"

IX

arrive at the intersection
with the statue of Joseph Hodges Choate (1832 - 1917)
"lawyer, statesman, patriot" (wonder — any relation
to the Choate School? — wonder what do you
have to do to be a patriot?)

call to mind, recite:

Mary Estey's Petition

The humbl petition of mary Easty unto his Excellencyes Sr. W. Phips and to the honourd Judge and Bench now Stting in Judicature in Salem and the Reuerend ministers humbly sheweth.

That wheras your poor and humble Petition being condemned to die Doe humbly begg of you to take it in your Judicious and pious consideration that your Poor and humble petitioner knowing my own Innocencye Blised be the Lord for it

and seeing plainly the wiles and subtility of my accusers by myselfe cannot but Judg charitably of others that are going ye same way of myself

if the Lord stepps not mightily in I was confined a whole month upon the same account that I am condemed now for and then cleared by the afflicted persons as some of your honours know and in two dayes time I was cryed out upon by them and have been confined and now am condemed to die

the Lord aboue knows my Innocencye then and likewise does now as att the great day will be known to men and Angells —

I Petition to your honours not for my own life for I know I must die, and my appointed time is sett but the Lord he knowes it is that if it be possible

no more Innocent blood may be shed which undoubtidly cannot be Avoydd In the way and course you goe in

I question not, but your honours does to the uttmost of your Power in the discouery and detecting of witchcraft and withches

and would not be gulty of Innocent blood for the world

but by my own Innocencye I know you are in the wrong way the Lord in his infinite mercye direct you in the great work if it be his blessed will that no more Innocent blood be shed I would humbly begg of you that your honors would be pleased

to examine theis Afflicted Persons strictly and keep them apart some time and Likewise to try some of those confesing witches I being confident there are seuerall of them as belyed themselves and others as will appeare if not in this word I am sure in the world to come whither I am now agoing and I Question not but

youle see an alteration of thes things

they say myselfe and others haueing made a League with the Diuel we cannot confesse I know and the Lord knows as will shortly appeare they belye me and so I Question not but that they doe others

the Lord aboue who is the Searcher of all hearts knows that as I shall answer it att the Tribunall seat that I know not the least thinge of witchcraft

therefore I cannot

I dare not belye my own soule

I beg you honers not to deny this my humble petition from a poor dying Innocent person and I Question not but the Lord will giue a blesing to yor endeurs.

— Essex County Court Records

X

turn right on Boston St.

— the main road

to Peabody, stroll through seedier surroundings —
dirty, unkempt buildings, "Pilgrim Diner,"
"Arge's Liquors," "Sunshine Coin Laundromat,"
"Sports Haven Bar" featuring Miller's High Life,

(think of sport,

of the swaying High Life — of the afflicted,
the possessed, who, as they later confessed,
did it for "sport" —

wipe more sweat from your brow,

find shade to jot down notes — "Dunkin Donuts,"
"Right lane must turn right" and "Yard sale today,
August 28, 1993" (as at the great day will be known
to men and angels) "antiques, books, tools,
household items, etc,"

Note all this alongside an entry

from the *History of Topsfield*, p.90, the display
in "'the hall' usually on open shelves,"
the "pride of the housewife — the dress
of pewter and latinn ware,"

all this below

the spectre of new red brick buildings
with square black hole windows: Salem Heights
Condominiums looming over the roof of the laundromat,

XI

take a left onto Pope Street, start up
the incline, judging charitably of others
going the same way as ourselves, offering
them our arm as we depart from the baseball field,
the lower half of "Gallows Hill Park,"

get short of breath

walking up the three foot wide asphalt path
to the top of the hill, to the playground,

look up, read from the Towne family record —
"Mercifully, the deaths of William and Joanna [Towne]
occurred before the mad witchcraft trials began
and they did not have to suffer through the trials
of their three daughters which included excommunication
from the church and the disgrace and pain of executions."

read the petitions of old Isaac Estey whose life
dragged on until 1712, the myriad petitions
to clear his wife's name, presented again
and again to the presiding legislature,

(imagine the families' long trek down
this winding trail, the eight dark scarecrows
silhouetted against the red sunset,

the Reverend Noyes'

"Eight firebrands of Hell" ringing
in their ears . . .

four little words . . .

echoing . . .

still echoing off the pavilion,

the chipped paint, the white pillars,
and black shingled roof)

XII

observe the large juts
of rock rising out of the sere brownsward,
the broken glass glittering in sunlight —
the small fires on grey slate
and packed brown grass,

the basketball court (well kept up)
and a tall flagpole, the stars and stripes
streaming over all —

over the bare-chested young man,
sitting on the 15 x 9 oblong cement slab,
radio blaring,
the young man looking out
over Salem, the factory with two smokestacks,
and the new condominiums —
(tomorrow —
on the slab, we'll see an alteration
of these things, we'll see an empty six pack,
a used hypodermic needle, and three quarters,
three shining pieces of silver,
we'll see

the graffiti: DEATH STORM
BRINGER)

but today, the present, look,
look there in the clearing, in the shade,
a pre-school climber, with clean, cool steel rungs,

look clearly at the landscape after the storm
at the apology of Thomas Perkins and all
the repentant jurors who
"hereby signify to all in general, and to
the surviving sufferers in special, our deep sense of, and sorrow for, our errors . . . for which we are much disquieted and distressed in our minds, and do therefore humbly beg forgiveness . . . and do declare, according to our present minds, we would none of us do such things again, on such grounds, for the whole world,"

XIII

and, at the end . . .

                                        know that
Mary Estey "when she took her last farewell
of her husband, children, and friends, she was,
as is reported by them present, as serious, religious,
distinct, and affectionate as could well be expected,
drawing tears from the eyes of almost all present"

and feel sad, if you must,

not for Mary Estey who could not, dared not
belie her soul,

                                                  but for
                                                           Stoughton
and all other unrepentant judges —

          the patchwork of their sere spirits
          stretched tight across the rungs,
          drying as long as words last . . .

and for ourselves, our countrymen, our race,
our species,
                    for how little we have learned,
how little we have accomplished —

not for Mary Towne Estey, the self forgetful,
or for anyone else who has (as the searcher
of all hearts knows)
                                        only love —
no trace of bitterness — in the heart.

Judge Corwin's Bedroom

on the second floor,
the most private, the warmest
room of the house —
                                        a loft
with the huge three door
captain's chest that held his socks,
his shirts, his shorts,

the antique (even then)
black well-preserved Bible box —
saving for generations, the news,

and the canopy bed
with hand-sewn quilt
and feather mattress —
                                        so soft

where he sat,
an authority on guilt,
in Salem, in 1692, a head,

a chairman of sorts,
fiddling with his vest,
conducting interviews

of the chosen,
the candidates-elect.

Judge Corwin's Kitchen

large beams, white plaster walls —
and pewter dishes on a Venetian red table —
the top of which turns over into a chopping board,

a brass pot, a churn, and butter molds
with hand carved wooden heads, a cheese press,
and bowls with beans and corn,

a huge black stone fireplace
with a large hot coal oven in back,
iron cooking utensils hung on a rack
above — with a musket and powder horn,

the fireplace — tended in succession
by each of his three wives — the folds
of their long muslin skirts swirling
dangerously close to the hearth,

(more women, many more colonial women
died from burns when their clothes
accidently caught fire than were hanged
as witches)

and there — in the far corner, yet
on the other side of the depression,
three centuries away from the trial,
rocking in its toy cradle,

a rag doll, a poppet,
with a strange stitched smile.

The Flax Break

painted Venetian red (iron rust mixed
with sour milk) — beside the larder,

among the odd, old things,
in Judge Corwin's kitchen —

a wooden contraption for treating
the rough, unruly flax — in 1692 —

a dual process in Salem — first pound
with hammer, into mush with no name,

then comb the crushed material through
the sharp points of the carder,

and voila! the flax is fixed,
stretched harp strings

under duress on an antique frame,
strings ready to sound, to resound,

ready to make fine linen.

Leatherman's Cave

The Mattatuck Trail, at the southeast base
of Crane's lookout, narrows to a rock hallway,
a birth canal,
                                    the blue arrow on
the rust orange rock reassuring, yes
this is the trail; this way please,
bow your head, mull over the prose,
the guidebook lines on his story:

> *His name was Jules Bourglay; he was born*
> *near Lyons, France. He worked for his prospective*
> *father-in-law, who owned a prosperous leather*
> *business. His market miscalculations ruined*
> *the business, and he was rejected by his betrothed.*
>
> *These losses affected his mind, and he left France*
> *and came to the new world around 1862 and spent*
> *his last twenty-seven years alone, walking*
> *in his roughly oval circuit between*
> *the Connecticut and Hudson Rivers . . .*

bow your head, twist sideways
as you enter through the same crevice
that the leatherman, that eccentric wanderer
who roamed old Indian trails, in summer
and winter, in sickness and in health, entered
every 34th night for over twenty-seven years —
this one, just one of 34 caves along his route,

this crevice, opening into an odd room
with a pillar in the center —
the bedroom/kitchen of the rock house,

look at the charred remains of a campfire
in the alcove, beneath the natural air shaft
chimney, a passage through the overhang,
the strange orange roof studded with chunks
of white marble, the slight opening
through which a man resting after his day's walk
in his sixty pounds of crudely laced leather clothes
          (his two leather bags — with all
          his worldly possessions — placed safely
          at the foot of his stone bed)
through which a man who could not be persuaded
to sleep in a house or barn could clearly see
the shadows of the changing trees, the lights
of the unchanging stars.

Then step over the threshold into the arrowhead
living room, the rock chairs, the natural skylight,
and small crack of window through which you see
the two pronged branch of a dead tree, a silver
tuning fork pointing forward to talk radio, to TV
and back to the man who slept with rattlesnakes
(his favorite companions), and begged food
and tobacco by gestures, never speaking,
but expressing his thanks with grunts,

and scramble down the mini cliff
of slanting rock into the last room, the study
with a fresh air view where the visitor
can lean against the rough stone, survey
his surroundings, the rock floor and walls,
the gray black streaked with orange and flecks
of glittering iron pyrite (fool's gold)

check out the blue marker — still on
the trail of something, something drifting
away like wisps of early morning mist,
something akin to peace or married bliss,
a distant cousin of redemption,

that the leatherman found long before
his escape from the hospital and his last sleep
in a cave in Ossining, NY,

. . .

step out of the cave into the late 20th
century sunlight, take in the view,
the breath-taking view of acres
of fire ravaged trees before the long
serpentine strips of super highway
speckled with traffic moving
in opposite directions,
                                        and begin the steep
rugged descent down the stark cliff —

the wisps gone, the jagged edge
looking as if the whole face of the mountain
had been blown away.

The Economics Professor Visits St. John,

arrives on the ferry from St. Thomas, finds
2/3 the island a National Park (donated
by the Rockefeller family) with two campgrounds —
one, privately owned with "L" shaped tents
on platforms of seasoned wood;

he unpacks, finds himself
walking down a dirt road — a long, narrow dirt road,
finds himself drawn like a metal filing
toward a magnet,

toward the pole,
the stone column in the center of the clearing
with an old broken windmill on top,
the old sugar mill;
he finds himself standing there
on the cliff looking down — not at the white sand,
the Caribbean, the snorkelers, the dots and dashes
of bright colors, the flecks in the clear blue —

but at the more somber
view, the dark, half-hidden wall on the ledge
below, a mosaic of local shells and rocks
marking an old trail from the slaves' living quarters
to the mill — to the circular path round
and around the mill, where people and horses
were whipped and walked round and around —

grinding the cane
startled
by the dark forms writhing up out of old ruts,
spirits rising, like mist from the earth,
like steam from old kettles —

the grey-brown fog
condenses into liquid, then solid form,
takes distinct human shape,
their features
become clear;
their eyes, deep wells
brimming with thousands of years of human misery . . .

Lines Started Outside Filene's Basement

on the second floor of the Worcester Center Mall, 7:15 pm, March 3, 1991 while waiting for my wife and her sister to try on dresses and looking over the mostly deserted stores, at the chain curtains let down so the merchandise (what's left of it) cannot get out — thinking of the clerks behind bars in their darkened stores counting their meager take while I'm sipping my ice and diet soda from Orange Julius (the only other store open) instead of coffee, which the attendant had warned me off of, saying: "It's pretty bad. It's been sitting around for a while," all else closed, even Jordan Marsh, the increasingly barren, sinking flagship with its 40% off going out of business sale — watching every once in a while a person going up or down the escalator, an eerie, quiet depressing depression scene overall, everything in decline, even

the fountain appears tired, worn out, only half
its lights on, the emerging water forms:
puny, gurgling, hunch-backed wraiths
half-heartedly attempting to escape —

being interrupted

by the well-dressed middle-aged man with the slight British accent asking for a match (which of course I don't have) no light, no connection to the black teen with his baseball cap on backwards and his back to the fountain while facing the square of light that is Filene's Basement and inhaling his cigarette — feeling no connection to the young white with the scruffy beard who wanted to stay but left with the fat hispanic woman who said: "I'm going!" and meant it! "What's up, Jack?" he offered in passing "Not much," I replied as friendly as I could, "Nice hat!" he said, already passed, "Thanks," I replied to his receding shape — and thinking the parking costs $10.00 to get into this place.

Lines Written Hungry, with a Severe Headache, Jouncing along the Deagan

With every jounce, the nerve ends twinge.
My stomach growls; the body
is in revolt — O.K., body,
this is between you and me.

Your throb is counterpoint
to my imagination, keeps me
from being lost in pictures on old urns
or in songs of golden birds
in too, too distant palms.

You force me to use you 'n jam
your throbbing into the rhythm
of natural speech.

Yes, you force me to use exact change only,
to follow the directions of the toll booths'
three green lights shimmering "Go!"
on the black, rain-slicked pavement.

Go on —

Look up — 1/2 hr after sunset, see
the last gray light wind through storm clouds.
See the pale stream cascade over black rocks
past real trees on the shore. Go on —

Kneel in the darkening shade,
drink deep from cupped hands
dipped in the pink-flecked bay.

666 POET

reads the license plate; Satan
is glowing;
                    the righteous birds
are chirping,
                    attacking the windshield.

My son, of course, went 0-5
(with 3 K's) the night
                              I first thought
of this poem, and his error
in the ninth lost the key game.

The pump of the community well
has broken,
                    and no one can fix it;
just dry rusty dust
                              coughs
up out of the pipes,
                              and the cows
in the pasture behind my house
are off schedule and giving
radioactive milk.
                    The built up tooth
on top of one of my root canals
has chipped off;
                    the other canal
is infected; both
                    have to be redone, and

the newspaper says the eggs
of all the chickens in Connecticut
contain twice the cholesterol
of the national average
                              while overhead
the ozone layer is depleting faster
than even the most pessimistic
had imagined —
                    the cancer rate
is skyrocketing — Wheeeee!

Once a month my front lawn
is a carpet of snakes,
                              slithering,
dancing — their eyes glittering
in the light of the full moon.

Orpheus Greeting the Dawn

(*while waiting for the birth*
of Aidan FitzGerald Scrimgeour,
May 28, 1995)

at the Elvehjem Museum of Art,
Madison, Wisconsin, holding your hand —

the massive dark head of shade trees
with small squinting eyes of light,
appears as a natural outgrowth,
as part of the dark shore, framing

an oval pool of the purest white sky.

Orpheus stands, back to us, facing
the trees, his head, his lyre,
his outstretched hand, in the pool
of light above the line of mountains,

his offerings to the fire in the sky,
the god he worships above all others.

You squeeze my hand; the shore contracts;
the distant temple trembles, the trees
begin the dance of delivery,

the dance of the beginning of the world.

The Isthmus

on the way to Picnic Point,
with Lake Mendota on the right and left
and trail before and behind

trail through overcast drizzle,
where we walked carefully over and around
the slippery wet clay,

and trail up an incline, where the land
swells, broadens, and there is room
for all kinds of diversions, side paths
for views and reviews,

until we get to the point, the anticlimactic
point with a man sitting on a bench, writing —

the point, where we are out of place, intruders,
feeling the gnats and mosquitos, watching
the grey cloud covered water for miles around —

the grey seeping in.

We snap a couple of pictures,
then leave,
                    start the return, as everything
awakens, the clouds lighten, the birds' songs
become louder, more varied, the turtle's head
comes out of his shell, the baby ducks appear
magically behind their mother,

and when we reach the isthmus — the stem,
the umbilical cord between seed and blossom,
between two worlds, one poem and the next,

the sun explodes like a flash bulb,
etches our embrace in lines of memory
and anticipation,

the lake shimmering
as far as our eyes can see.

James Madison Park, May 30, 1995

returning from our walk,

strolling past couples sitting
on the stone wall, facing the faint glow
in the west, after sunset over the lake,

past people in small clusters talking,
basketball players still shooting around
after the last game, a family packing up
their things from a picnic table, past

Frisbees flying, settling into outstretched
hands or into the darkening grass,

past the square-dancing in the chapel, people
of assorted colors, shapes and sizes framed
in the open doorway — the light
the music, the laughter floating off —

                                                            spores
carrying a vision of the way
life could be,
                                                spores drifting
in the wind.

Bryant Park: New York, July 1995

I

Tall, thin trees — smooth, stately, khaki clad
with occasional elbow patches of peeled bark and limbs
not even starting till 25-30 ft up — trees competing
with skyscrapers for sun, and rising on both sides
of the inlaid stone path — their intertwined branches
forming a green canopy over the people strolling
to the public library, to the outdoor cafe, over

the people ambling to and fro, sitting on benches,
on chairs, people relaxing, playing chess
in the mottled shade,
over the 4 pigeons
walking down the center of the path, scattering
when humans approach, then reclaiming the center
as if the walk were naturally, rightfully theirs . . .

the light breeze flutters the leaves overhead,
the sleeves of my San Francisco T shirt,
the beds of wrinkle leaved ivy, turns them
into small pools with dark green waves, rippling . . .

the breeze feels good on bare skin in the shade,
cool, soothing . . .

II

A tall angular black man, sits upright on a bench,
sleeping, his left elbow on his thigh, his left palm,
a pillow supporting his ear, the left side of his head —
the head tilted at a strange almost 90 degree angle —

another man, with plastic cup in outstretched hand
approaches passersby left and right, asking softly,
with just a trace of menace: "Can you help me out?"

the chess hustler with the sheepish smile, the soft voice
with a slightly foreign accent, the "how did I ever manage
to do that" look as he pockets the $ 5.00 — the "Good game!"
to everyone he beats.

and finally, an older
once attractive woman in a partially unbuttoned,
dirty print blouse, a once white ribbon
in her stringy, greying hair,

a slightly distracted
woman carrying a plastic bag with all her belongings
gets a cupful of water from the public fountain,
washes her face, and fills her canteen —

all the while shaking her head —
her head moving up and down,

back and forth
in short jerky motions

as if she were talking to somebody,
her mouth moving in and out like a fish underwater,
like an infant who still thinks the earth is alive.

War Game

"Pow!
pow! pow! pow!
pow! pow!"
toy plastic gun
"Pow! pow!"
in hand "Pow!"
smiling "Pow!"
tall, blonde, blue-eyed
"Pow! pow! pow!"
3 year old boy
"Pow! pow!"
stands there
"Pow! pow! pow!"
continually "Pow!"
killing me "Pow pow! pow!"

Reeling back
"Pow! pow!"
in pain "Pow!"
I ask "Pow!"
Why "Pow! pow!"
do you want
"Pow! pow!"
to hurt me
"Pow! pow! pow!"
why "Pow!"
do you want
"Pow!" to kill
"Pow! pow! pow!"
He answers
"Pow! pow!"
I likta kill people
"Pow! pow! pow!"

Silenced "Pow! pow!"
I brush back
"Pow!" strands of hair
"Pow! pow!"
rub my forehead
"Pow! pow! pow!"

Whatsa matta
"Pow! pow!" he asks
"Pow! pow! pow!"
ya gotta headache?
"Pow! pow! pow! pow! pow!"

This Morning

turned on the radio
to check on the snow warnings,
the cancellations,
          hoping for a delayed opening,

          finding instead 6 yr old Eduardo, dead
                    on arrival — while Sally, his mother
                    and two other children escaped
                    with minor injuries.

"that's Eduardo," you said, "the one
from Head Start, who learned so much
in one year — my success story.

               — he was so proud
when he learned his colors — 'Eduardo's
wearing red!' he said, beaming"

                         . . . later
          in the faculty dining room
          hearing about the driver of the pick up —
          that plowed into their car from behind,
          his 9 dwi arrests,
                    and of the tough sergeant,
          blood all over his arms and chest,
          pale as a ghost, shaking, mute . . .

no words to express this . . .

Challenger

The quarter moon,
a Cheshire Cat smile,

curls, cozies up, appears glued
at some odd angle to the Empire State Building,

hangs suspended a few inches above
the sharp spikes of skyline.

The Empire towers stories above it,
layers upon layers of squares —

some lit up, some dark, all supporting
red warning lights aspiring to the stars.

Minutes pass — then nothing, nothing but
that building, more buildings, and blank night sky . . .

the smile disappeared in space
like debris in the sea.

Ant

1/8 of an inch long — after
crumbs of oat bran

muffins — my middle finger
squishes you on the beige

table — you're still
alive, squirming (not enough

pressure, thinks I) I
squish you again — index

finger this time, harder,
more prolonged, still after

release, you stand on end —
defiant, alive 'til

the final squish and flip
onto the white sill — now

a black speck — drying
in the sun.

Human Brain: Figure 11.1

in the biology teacher's handout —
three views — the "inferior"
shows a praying insect, antennae
outstretched — trapped in the wrinkles
of a walnut shell

the "lateral," long distance view
shows a mushroom cloud arising
out of the cerebellum, the dark
hooded executioner's face half hidden
by the white stem,

and the "sagittal," the close up
where the cerebrum hovers over all,
the pineal body is visible above
the fourth ventricle, and the cerebellum
is simply delicious,
                              a sliced mushroom
sauteed with onions in vegetable oil.

The Dredging Machine

looks like something out of Mark Twain —
a clean white John Deere cab
and two black smokestack cylinders —

a mini-steamboat,

a huge floating vacuum cleaner — bloody red
intestine pipes curling above black pontoons,

and the long flexible thick black hose, a tail
trailing from the ship's rear,
disappearing
into the bay and reappearing as a long
black snake gliding out of the sea,

a snake spewing
dredged sand on top of the large dune
at the center of Tern Island —

the dune, the island — protected seashore,
endangered terns' eggs, etc. being groomed
by the bright yellow dozer.

They are enlarging the island —
"changing the course," they call it —
protecting
the shorefront real estate, the fishing industry,

and (oh, yes) destroying the terns
in order to save them.

Terns' Nesting Area: Do not Disturb

reads the sign, "Walk along
the beach only." That's O.K.
with me. It's peaceful here alone
with the sand, the sea, and the shells
secreted away in my shirt pocket, the shells
gently chafing my chest.

Two miles down the shore — bathers,
beach umbrellas, ice chests, and portable toilets,
while here, playful waves send foam
to within six inches of my right foot,
planted firmly in the sand —
the heel dug in.

The mind sails off into yesterday — such fun;
the family swimming in the storm — no sun,
just kids bobbing like dolphins
in the gong-grey sea.

Today — everything so clear, way
way out in Buzzards' Bay, the red points
of sailboats scraping the blue sky
know nothing of me, these fragile shells,
this shore, these waves roiling down
into ripples tickling, lapping
at the edge of all endangered species.

Short Sands Beach: York, Maine, August 1983

6:00 AM

The ocean, an eternity
of diffuse pink slight waves,
washes over our bare toes, soothes
the pain of your mother's death.

We look up, can't tell
whether it's grey cloud under pink sky
or pink cloud over grey sky; we can't tell
whether the sun has risen.

Two gulls ease toward the rocks
at the base of the cliff. The sun
leaks through cloud bars. Gold sequins
dance on the rippling grey gown.

8:00 AM

We nestle in the gull's rocks, watch
the waves thrust themselves into crevices,
then cascade in playful waterfalls, back
into foam, back into eddies in the sea.

The sun — suddenly free,
sears off the gown. The sequins
become schools of fireflies
flickering on grey flesh, flickering
in grey space, become thousands
of little meteors, little comets
chasing their own tails, thousands
of little suns — set burning,
etching a special breakfast
on the rippling slate table —

each sun — a dish, a disc, a world, a brief flame
dying as soon as it is born.

Breakwater Beach: November 1993

on the driftwood log bench
in the midst of grass tresses blowing
in 70 degree November wind — enjoying the hum
of creation, the bustle of 7 year old Nicholas and
his father on their hands and knees — building,
playing in their great network of tunnels, roads,
castles, moats and assorted mounds of dry and wet sand —

their world! their civilization! —
complete
with a steam-shovel and a fleet of yellow trucks, towing,
releasing loads
here and there,

and the long deep channel,
scraped out with a sharp stick and bare hands,
enticing the sea to visit this child's world, to come
with her small bay waves in tow,
an invitation she
accepts, yet responds to less and less often, knowing
her limitation —
she sends through the trench
smaller and ever rarer spurts, smoothing, grooming
the floor of the tunnels,
until it is time to leave,
to give in —
time for the unexpected reprieve —

for us — the impromptu present of the very day —
the glistening sands,
the moats, and mounds,
the roads and tunnels,
the castles
for us to play and live in . . .

evening will come soon enough — night sounds
will echo in the vacant air —
there will be
time to wash it all away.

Memorial Day, 1996: The Bridge

Standing on the solid bridge —
the hollow sound of our walking sticks
echoing off the wooden planks

over the Shepaug River — the bridge
supported by 9 inch square timbers
bolted into cement and rock, built

by land trust volunteers, whole families
working together, so enthused
they forgot their regular jobs —

her son was the engineer, she says,
her husband perhaps the most excited,
most involved in the project,

in rolling the bridge on logs,
hoisting it into place with a crane —
his surprised cry when it slipped

off once and marooned the dog
on the far shore — the same dog,
years older but still with us today

as three (no longer four) human bodies
and one intermingled human spirit tingling
on the bridge watch sunlit foam

swirl past in the current, the slight
dizzying sensation, the illusion
of movement, the mind sailing

through thin air, the spinning leaf
green sea, beyond past and present, life
and death — the bruise purple clouds

downstream, behind us.

Walking up Corne Neck Road

parallel to the shore, looking
in the direction of the sea —

light green dunes, wild roses, gulls,
smoke signal clouds drifting off

from a red diamond holding its ground
in the center of the blue sky,

a lone red kite,
                              held by invisible string,
above the invisible sea,

the invisible beach, the people walking,
perhaps running, in the sand.

Mohegan Bluffs

I

From the Tourist Bench,

                                                  high on the cliff
the near bluff appears as a large forehead
with green bushy hair, a forehead brooding over

black rock, a bridge of nose on which
the body of one of the forty Mohegan warriors
may have caught and hung over 500 years ago

over the two curved eyebrows of shoreline
where the specks of an American family at play
are small mites, irritants in the left eye,

the two kids skimming stones into the sea.

II

On the Shore,

                                                  a mite, myself,
sitting on a small hunchback rock,
my bare feet ensconced in pebbles, waves
massaging my toes, ankles,
                                                                  then receding,
the tow pulling the pebbles over and around —
playfully tickling my feet,
                                                                  the sound
of a boy's marbles clicking in a cloth bag.

• • •

The sudden, violent wave, the chill
of cold water over my crotch, my breast . . .

the receding rocks scraping my feet . . .

and the withdrawal sound — stone dice
shaking in a steel fist, the rattle
of dead men's bones.

III

The Sinister, Seemingly Playful,

seductive sound
of waves over rocks, the insistent jive
of a hustler who knows that before long
this cluster of cliffs will rest in a bed
on the ocean floor,
that before long
Block Island (and Manhattan) will disappear
like Atlantis,
and the Southeast Lighthouse
(moved grudgingly inch by inch to the top
of Mount Greylock)
will warn vacationing mariners
of the approaching Adirondacks —
the hustling waves,
bobbing, nodding, like the head
of a chess master who sees mate in seven.

IV

I Enter Through the Mouth

of an old dried up river bed, climb through
the windpipe, and emerge in an Edenic land,
where the young pink and white granite rocks
lie peacefully in the wild grass, in the sun,
like sleeping lambs . . .

and loll amidst them, see
at my feet a 3 and 1/2 inch wide stream
trickle towards home . . .

resting, dreaming, looking back
and up toward the source — noting, there,
above the rim — the corner of the tourist bench,

evidence of mind . . .
looking out and down the pipe,
through the sights, through two huge grey clay sentinels
to the pebble strewn beach, the foam, the black
baptized rocks, the waves, and beyond —

to the rocks smothered with the sea's green slime,
and to the sea, itself, as it is, as it was, and
will be for some time.

V

With My Back to the Sea,

pausing,
1/2 way up (or down) the 151 steps
put in (they say) just two years ago,
leaning into the railing,
looking into the gully,

in pure sunlight,
the hillside with occasional patches
of shining ocher grass —

and the bright, light green leaves
of sprawling blueberry bushes (peopled
by hard dots of unseen, unripened fruit)

and at the center, amidst a gathering
of wild blooming roses, one old, grey rock

peeps out, awakening.

In the Sun

I

As we approach, walking the beach
from Mohegan Bluffs toward the southwest point,
the grey formation appears as a horse's head
in profile, but when we arrive, rest
under the clay overhang which offers
no relief from the two o'clock sun,
the horse is gone — transformed into a giant
shark with scars where there once were eyes
and runes on the inside of his throat — his nose
tilted upward in the 90 degree heat, aims
straight through the light haze, this arrowhead —

this simple, direct, pointed adoration of the sun!

II

just resting on a flat rock in the stark
sun, soaking in the heat — too hot for sex,
yet enjoying the love play of sea and rocks,
the lapping of the waves, the sunlit foam
gurgling over and around a trinity of dark
glistening stones —

                                        not sure whether
the tide is going out or coming home,
but knowing whenever the waves push themselves
in the crevices between the rocks we'll hear
the oohs and aahs of withdrawal, the tickling
chatter of small stones pouring over each other,
colliding in chance encounters of delight —

curling over and around the syllables
of your question: "What is Love?"

III

and to the right, another clay rock head
with sealed slanted eyes and nose turned up
parallel to the shark's, the nose repelled
by the smell of human sweat, the faint odor
of flesh and blood,

                                        a clay stranger
blaming the sun, the silent words issuing
through cracked frowning lips: "the sun
baked me this way;

the sun made me not do it."

IV

in the distance — the mariner's bane,
the infamous black rock — half in
half out, stark block at low tide
in daylight, invisible at high tide
or in the night sea —

blackened as if broiled, charred by the sun
though we know, when we stop to think,
the sea and its slime are to blame

• • •

and on top of this rock — one
black and white gull, alone
in the center, watching the tide,
his dark side matching the rock,

his warning white feathers ablaze
in the fierce light of the sun.

The Seedless Orange on the Beach

a spot of color, a hybrid,
just out of the waves' reach,

discarded fruit preening

amidst a few dark plum-sized stones
casually strewn around a drab expanse
of sand —

                    the seedless orange —

a sun in a sand-brown void
surrounded by scattered fragments
of asteroid and bones —

Sand Dollars

round shells with a flower design
imprinted on their humped backs,

and the veins in their underbellies,
branching out of the hole that sandpipers

so neatly drill before sucking out
the juiciest flesh morsels, so many,

strewn on the strip of Ocean Beach —
large ones, small ones, dirty ones

clean ones, gray ones, cream ones,
some tinged with black, some with green,

such abundance, you can't pick them all —
your hands, your pockets full —

you're sure you've gathered more
than you'll ever need, or spend . . .

'til settled in your study — 3000 miles
from the Pacific, you miss the ones

given away, mourn the ones broken
in transit, survey the chips in all

the survivors' edges, and hear the echo
of small white bones — dove wings

fluttering in the vacant shell.

Salt Marsh

stalks of androgynous yellow-green-
brown grasses glisten

in morning sunlight — wade
in high tide — swaying, bending,

some going under, some with their tops
snapped, their heads bowed

at a sharp angle —
like herons, like swans.

Daffodils

The 1/2 mile or so of roadside at the entrance
to the White Conservation Center, an impressive
stretch of genetic engineering —

so many deviants, so many shades of yellow
and white with an occasional splash
of orange,
                                        all coming
out of the same aqua-green leaves and stems —

the outside petals in four basic colors:
deep afternoon yellow, dominant noon sun,
pale sun in fog, and recessive white of moon —

four colors swaying together, waltzing
                                        in tune to the music
of the inner trumpets of varying dimensions,
some long, thrusting out of the center, blaring,
vibrating,
              some medium, open to the wind,
                            some little more
than buttons, quarter and dime sized,
mainly orange buttons, legal tender
without gender, speaking most eloquently
in sweet, clear tones —

the hearts of all denominations dancing together
with the flesh — not only yellow on yellow,
white on white, but bright yellow on pale or dark,
or white —

or white or pale or dark yellow on all shades —

                                                  all combinations
in harmony with the music of the spheres, the song
emanating from all colors, all shapes and sizes,
the high clean notes straight from the core,

from each and every one of the flock
gamboling in the May breeze.

Snails

The yellow-brown and dull ocher seaweed
matted on the rock still looks like a walrus
emerging from primeval sea,
                                        lord over
the grey-white guano and hundreds of snails
clinging to damp rock and golden hemp strings,

                                        over snails —
both those that had held tightly and clung
to their place on the underside of rocks
and those that had not, those that were flung,
deposited here and there by the sea —

over a colony of small beige-grey lumps
that move when you least expect them —

snails moving so slowly,
1/4 inching up that glistening strand,
or down that slope into that crevice

leaving a trail of shining slime behind them
on the black rocks . . .

                                look there —
rolling over in that bed of sleaze, on weed
that looks like stems of plastic flowers,
no blooms, just noodles of rubber that bounce back
when squeezed —

there — those two, locked
in an embrace.

The Starlings

ugly dark brown
speckled birds, native
to England, "brought overseas"

(says the Biology Professor)
"by some moron who thought
they were cute" — small

chunky survivors that nest
in holes the size
of a 10 yr old's fist

odd holes, any holes
where old rusted pipes
have been ripped out

like that one in the
brick wall on the far side
of Higgins — they drive

away the bluebirds,
and woodpeckers as Puritan
settlers repelled

the Narragansett
and the Wampanoags —
starlings,
long yellow-beaked birds

filled with alien song
and glistening with iridescence
when the sun strikes them right.

"V" Formation

There is a gap in the "V" formation
of autumn geese heading south.

The foliage glistens with radiant sunlight;
my oldest son, J.D., is singing
Woody Guthrie's "Deportees"

> *The crops are all in; the peaches are rotting,*
> *the oranges piled in their creosol dung.*

The reds, the yellows, the oranges mix
with the remaining green — the leaves,
breathtaking, hanging on, refusing to fall.

> *Who are those friends all scattered like dry leaves?*
> *The radio says they are just deportees.*

Was it twenty years ago he serenaded us
from the well of the old VW as we drove
along these same roads, through these same leaves
from graduate student housing to visit Yiayia?

Now, J. D., following Arlo's rendition — yes

> *. . . scattered like dry leaves*
> *all over the topsoil . . .*

Woody, Arlo; J. D., me; red, orange; green, yellow —
swirling, blent in an autumn rainbow.

> *My father's own father,*
> *he waded that river . . .*

"Hey, that's a great line," says J. D.
"Ya, I know," says I.

We look up and the gap is closed.
The "V" formation is solid — heading
into the twenty-first century and beyond.

At Dusk

a young man and woman stand at the far
edge of the pale rumpled beach — bare
feet firm in the shifting sand —

stare past the piled rocks, the remains
of a breaker, into the distance, as, more
than a long wedge offshore, one dark boulder
appears and disappears from sight —

two figures in shorts and T shirts,
standing close together, his left shoulder
touching her right, their opposite arms
straight, merging into one thin sapling
trunk growing out of intertwined roots,
out of one ten fingered hand —

before them the wide, wide ocean, the ever
dwindling light, the ever darkening waves,
breaking, bowing to them, laying bouquet
after bouquet of sparkling white
champagne foam at their feet.

Crow Lake

The crows row home in the flowing air,
vanish, as the dusk evaporates into night,
as I slip away from earth in my two oared
boat through the parting shrouds, reeds,
the towering, admonishing cattail fingers
toward the embers, the light that lingers
on the barely moving water — out of nowhere
the moon, the stars appear, their faint light
glows silver for a while, then emigrates
to the September side of clouds. The wind dies
down. I lie still in the boat that lies
enveloped in the night, in silence, peace.
The sound of ripples, the tug of daily needs,
the coarse caws of crows become memories,
the faintest of echoes.
The world, unmoored,
drifts away; its rocks, its trees, its shore
dissolve into yesterday, last summer,
or centuries before.

Mohegan Bluffs: Revisited

I

The young couple
(with the baby sitting on the man's shoulders)
stands on the lookout platform,
peering
into the grey gruel fog, at the soggy beach,
the large rock sentinels, the larger clay creatures
guarding the entrance to a nether world inhabited
by the 40 Mohegan warriors who were thrown
(or forced to jump) from these cliffs
over 500 years ago,

these guardians looming up out of the misty depths . . .

the young couple (with the baby riding the man's shoulders)
leaves — just as we arrive,
just as it starts to rain.

II

They leave,
and we begin the descent down the long,
winding stairs to the beach.

The rain pelts us harder.
You wait, while I hurry
all the way to the bottom, jump from the last step
to the wet rocks, search briefly for shelter,
a cave, a recess in the cliffs,
find none, return,
meet you, poised, waiting — 1/3 the way down.

III

We stand, in profile, in the gusting wind
and rain, our fingers gripping the wire frame
of our large, ugly umbrella to keep it from flying
inside out — in profile, part of the somber scene,
our silhouettes merging with the umbrella,
the wet grey-black railing, the black bushes,
the beige clumps of matted grass on the dark
brown hillside —
lost in world-sadness,
one with the bleak foreground shapes and forms,
one with the ominous background, those 40 shades,
this deep brown hallowed earth, the overcast
and weeping sky.

Short Sands Revisited: August, 1985

I

The workmen in the new solar equipped houses
peer through wall length picture windows.

In full view, we sit, decorous,
on the rocks, holding hands,

looking out at dull clouds — nothing
but gray clouds and gray haze

over the numb sea.

II

Through how much mist, we wonder,
must the sun rise? How long?

O Lord, how long till the weary sun
declines to be born again?

James R. Scrimgeour

Birthday Poem

Breakfast at Ernie's at Old Harbor, six
people in cramped space—around a small
inside table—too hungry to wait for
an outside place with a view—blueberry
pancakes going down quickly—then lingering
over our second cups of coffee when
out of nowhere, the question: "what was your
favorite birthday?" and I had to think
about that one—
                                        we don't celebrate
birthdays much—anniversaries every 13th,
but no big deal on birthdays, except
maybe that one, July 29, 1963—the summer
before our wedding when we sat—parked
across from Chris's parents at 65 Charlton
Street, Southbridge, and our tears kept
streaming, kept pouring down while listening
to "I Can't Stop Loving You" on the radio
in the old Dodge that wouldn't start unless
we could roll it down some kind of hill.

Where Is the Place of the Heart

Where the Buddha is killed
nightly like a character
of a novelist, where that place
in space stores all of our
thoughts, and actions, where we
are taken back to adverbs
in dawn like ears, where the octagon
in sky revolves its dark candy
that is the heart, where Lear's
bloody eyes are wrapped
in the sea's tissues, where
Aristotle blows through a conch
across time to us, where we watch
this film, paying no real admission,
where giant's words reverberate
on green hills, where we are like
sad mute lanterns, ice up our
spines, we will remain.
Sweet weeping ravens we have
become. The rocks of civilization
on our poor backs, the dream walks
up one too many mountains.
The collages of still and blinding
light. Where? Where are we really?
Where are we going? Where. Where.

In the Fog

with mist beading on my glasses —
and feeling hundreds, perhaps thousands
of droplets on exposed skin,

my skin, my ego dissolving in the fog —
my consciousness attaching to hundreds,
perhaps thousands of drops of mist —

and drifting in a world with no shore.

I can faintly hear the roar of the first wave —

dimly see hundreds, thousands, perhaps millions
of tiny droplets inside its white cap —

barely feel the slight pressure
from your hand in mine.

The Fountain at Night

contains an interesting illuminated sculpture
rising out of the large wading pool —
three metal forms playing — bathing,
cleansing one another —
                                        three vaguely god-like
forms, one, slightly taller — the father.

The water — glowing, gurgling halos
out of and around the heads of the son
and the holy ghost — the water,
                                                    all foam
and fluid running playfully over smooth
surfaces, dividing around sharp projections,

                                        and leaping — shocked,
surprised — from the collection plates
in the center —
                              thin jets of fluid
issuing forth from the father's head —
parabolas, umbrellas over all.

Now when you think you have it, the sculpture,
explained, look again — see the absurd
umbrella of water — see the phony future
halos . . . the irrelevant metal past . . .
interesting only as necessary background . . .
dissolve . . .
                                        — see the fluid, the now,
the shining, surging, pulsing lines of force

— feel, after our late night walk,
our white feet fresh in the green water.

Who's Blind Round This House Anyway

Hey, honey, I can't find it. Are you
sure there's a can of soup left? Yes,
I've looked in the diagonal cupboard, checked
every single can. There's a lot of peas
and string beans, some tomato paste, but
no chicken noodle soup. Are you sure
we're not out of it? I've felt around
in all the corners, especially that dark
little pocket to the back and the left of the opening
where fingers slide in. Yes, I'm sure,
absolutely sure, it's not behind the string beans
or the tuna fish, especially the tuna fish.
I can see, you know.

So we gotta stop buying tuna fish, but
what's how many dolphins they kill
to make one can of tuna fish to do
with the missing soup, which I don't really need
anyway. I'll just munch some saltines. No,
I'm not playing hero, and I don't need your hand
to guide me, that is, unless
you really want to . . . Well, well,
what do you know? There it is —
behind the tuna fish, right where
you said it was — feels kinda good,
your hand on my hand on the last can
of chicken noodle soup, don't it?

Breaking the Bread

Our oat bran breakfast —
eight hours ago — is history

long since digested, and we are
in the window of yet another restaurant

hungry, so hungry — waiting —
we have only our coffee, ourselves,

and a wicker basket of fresh bread,
delicious warm bread dwindling

into one piece — the size, maybe
of a human fist,
                    which you take
in your hand, break the crisp crust,
pull the soft bread in two;
                              you
keep the smaller for yourself, leave
the larger morsel for me —

I sip, savor my coffee,
casually pick up the last piece,

break it, keep the smaller, etc.

— your turn, mine — rays of sunset,
curious, peer through the cold glass,

see a small white offering
on the red napkin — still

something there, something
shining — even now.

Sea Ledges: Double Chocolate Truffles, Sunrise, and You

We feed each other the truffles, check out the two gull shaped clouds hovering over the dark outline of the island, the Audubon Bird Sanctuary, over the blue beacon in the tower next to the silhouette of the abandoned weather station, the blue beacon blinking on and off every five seconds, while nearby, against the lightening sky we see a few live gulls circling in arcs — their cries mingling with the sound of large waves crashing against the rocks, the vivid reds and orange of sunrise, the lingering taste of chocolate as we try to distinguish things in our surroundings — are those distant "v"s a whole flock of gulls? are those strange vague monster shapes rocks? is that a boat just this side of the island with a fisherman sometimes standing, sometimes sitting in it?

the sky gets lighter and lighter, the brightest colors turn pastel — yes,
gulls, yes, rocks with crevices and projections appearing — yes,
it is a boat with people, the boat drifting sometimes closer,
sometimes farther away — yes, yes, yes, I realize
as our lips meet, taste the last traces of chocolate,
as the waves surge up and down on the rocks,
as the sun rises astride the blue beacon — look,

look at it now — an orange helium balloon
straining to lift the sanctuary, the island
and glowing an even brighter, more intense yellow
as it warms to the task —

still more gulls moving in still more arcs,
moving from rock to rock, from pole to pole,
as if the rocks were charged with electrical
current —
the sudden shock
of the gull's white feathers lit in sunlight,

wow! eee!

the water sprinklers next door go on —
small jets of water fly over the now
green lawn.

A Miracle

Vacation's over, but awake again at dawn
on the third floor, looking out and down
into overcast drizzle past the grass
and trees and clear deserted road
into the mall's parking lot.

I have been looking at the ocean
too long, so long the lot is a grey sea,
the light pole a ship's mast, that flattop
brown building across the way a pier,
those two or three dark cars,
small islands,

and the fisherman in the red shirt,
out there, is walking on water.

On the Lawn of Our Lady

of the Elms college a
maple leaf grace-

fully falls into
the center of *Spring*

and All, gently lies
upon Williams'

"death the barber"
poem, then rises

on its haunches,
drags its stem

so slowly across,
underlines a passage

in a puff, an acci-
dental puff of wind.

Just Returning

from my decaf and bagel w/cream cheese —
enjoying the clean spring sky and trees

in general when one thin straight Linden
in particular — one long thin grey trunk

presents me with a glowing oval explosion,
an idea, a light bulb, a spring lollipop

of white petals with lime green leaf flavoring
and bees buzzing in and among the blossoms

this one tree, a small balloon bursting before
the astonished telephone and computer lines

in the face of the vacant church.

The French Impressionist Idea

of painting the same tree (a wild apple, perhaps)
every day of the year — every day

different light, a few buds, a few petals more or less,
a few leaves, some scrawny fruit, green or red, on or off,
more or less, every day — the same different tree

for display in a gallery — 365 frames
for the human passersby to see
the still moving pictures of the changing tree
rooted in the same open place, in plain view
dressing and undressing herself

see the clear, thin coat of ice
snap, fall in slivers,
see the buds,
the first blush of color, emerge
from the bleak limbs,
see her gradually don
her filmy pink negligee,
which she (a few frames later)
so gracefully, so carelessly discards
in a pink circle — a silk carpet
as she steps out of blossom

into her summer green dress, the green
becoming fuller, rounder, a becoming
maternity dress — protective coloration
for the young, green, ripening fruit

until the burgeoning sweet white flesh
within the scarlet skin can no longer be hidden
by insufficient green leaves,

the delicious fruit which can only be picked
or fall to rot like the turning leaves,

the beautiful red, orange, yellow, and light brown leaves,
which she sheds slowly, deliberately, a striptease, she
so slowly (in the final frames) sheds her color, her senses,
her blood and flesh, yes, her very skin,
so slowly
she lets it all go, and stands stark, elemental,
just so —
remains oblivious of the wind, and of
the pure white covering from above.

Tulip Fields

Close up — just layers of colors — green, red,
green, white, pink, green, violet, burgundy,

light blue — step back and it opens up
like an accordion, a Japanese fan — we see

the landscape, the dark house, the trees,
the red and white tulips in green grass,

with clouds, violets, and brook — step back
a bit further, Monet's scene
                                        explodes —

the red tulips become blotches of three
blood red wounds — crucified arms and chest

of cream white body lying in the green field,
the dark house with the black roof becomes

a head hung in sorrow, nodding to one side
and flanked by stalks of blackened broccoli

sprout trees — dark ghost growths —
stark contrast with sunlight on white/

gray clouds sailing blithely overhead —
while beneath the bank, the violet border,

the stream flows peaceful, content, with leaves
vaguely resembling human bodies floating,

perhaps swimming in it.

The Carriage, Snowy Road to Honfleur

looking down the white snow packed road,
the level road between two buildings
and the slanting hill — house, shed and hill
buried in snow,

and blurs of confederate grey smoke ghost trees
standing guard in the distance,

the large building, a plain rectangular house,
with triangle snow roof and two clear spots,
two small dots — could be windows,
could be eyes, fearful, peering out,

at the small dark horse drawn carriage,
with an even smaller man, perhaps Monet,
himself, sitting in it, the carriage slightly
askew, tilted, like a hat clamped on a jaunty,
sauntering head,

the man turned sideways looking
at the rocks in the clear hillside . . .

the simple cold window-eyes peering
over the man's shoulder, trying to see
what he sees, the steep ascent, the rocks
set in the slanted hillside like gravestones,

but . . . even if they could turn as you and I,
could step back, survey the whole scene bathed
in pale light from the faint peach and light cream
sky hinting of a rising (or setting) sun,

even if they could turn (as we know he will)
to look down the road at the large snow covered,
squiggly-limbed tree, the glowing brain stuff oval
fed by dark capillary veins,
                                        the tree directly
in front of the horse's nose, in the center
of the painting, the tree christened
with light and snow,

even if they turned,
they could not see.

Impression Sunrise

The sun, an empty orange balloon,
with a silly smile face in the center of a grey
fog bank, hangs low over the river that divides
the land and empties into the sea — the river,
nearly in the center of Monet's painting, its mouth
open, and the reflection of the sun, a rippling
orange tongue sticks out from north to south
at the black rowboat, a rounded teaspoon,
with a dose of two beings in dark blue-green
coats, looking at both sides —
                                        the tongue,
a warning shot across the bow . . .

two clearly human beings in a boat,
the one clear image in the misty scene,

the two figures, one sitting at the core,
looking behind the tongue, down the throat
of the beast, taking in the foul breath, the fog,
the desolation, the war ravaged land, the dead
grasshopper stick lines on one shore,

the other standing, resting on his oar,
staring at the smokestacks of factories,
the telephone poles, the masts of vague ships
poking up out of the nether,
                                        staring
at the burning sphere in a blanket of clay,

noting connections, staking his claims
on the three columns of smoke, a trinity
of genies,

eerie magi on wobbly thin stork legs,

three lead-grey horsemen of the apocalypse,
now arising in the dirty, dull orange smog,

three silhouettes in the dawning flames.

Sunrise: the Peg Leg Inn, Rockport, MA, August 1994

Stretched horizontal across the center
of the frame,
— slanting slightly down —

a peach/orange/cream/salmon/pink crack
of sky lies between grey clouds and under
a lighter grey (soon pale blue) sky

a line of color floating above an island,
a flat barge of rock, above the sea harbor
shimmering ever so slightly — faint rose,

above the grey front lawn with shapes
of two chairs sitting on the far edge
before the still dark stone wall and the
still darker gazebo with its thin black
needlepoint pole tilted a bit to the left,

and the dark forms of lobster boats creeping
ever so slowly in spirals, laying their traps

just that side of two small sailboats
inching along this side of and parallel
to the dark paw and snout of Bearskin Neck
poking into the sunrise — the quaint clouds

opening, the widening sky
turning bright magenta

and you, my love, moving back and forth
from one window to another and then back
to the bed for different — all incredible
views of the birth of another day,

of the sea so slowly seeping into blue,
of the masonry, the fine stone work
of the walls, of the gazebo becoming clear,
the lawn ever so slowly becoming green,

and the dark rocks in the flowing grass
becoming silver — dolphins swimming ever,
ever so slowly across a green sea,

all the while the background cries
of gulls and the sound of waves lashing
and relashing the taut canvas shore.

"A perfect painting!" you say,
"Many perfect paintings," I reply

with an even greater appreciation of Monet

of Renoir, of the exploding white — all new
— forever new — "You've got to come —
look at it from here — with me,"

and the 6:00 am bells begin to chime . . .

Now, the sea is clear — except
for a single speck, a point in time,
a boat sailing straight out, an inverse "V,"
an arrowhead trailing twin white lines
in its wake, lines parallel to the reflection
of the risen sun,
                                to the burning
yellow/peach pipe-line painted down
the center of the most recent text,

parallel lines of fire and foam — tremulous
expressions of paint and poem —

conducting cords across the rippling sea.

Babson Farm Quarry

Mining abandoned in 1939 — the hoisting
machines, the derricks, the steam-powered
drills are gone, but the walls remain,
the smooth sliced stone walls still project
at odd angles into points — arrowheads
aimed outward toward various regions
of the universe or inward towards the center
of a large, spring-fed, blue-carpeted room

with no ceiling — couples, each with
a unique view, stand or sit on the tip
of most of the seven arrows pointing in —

our view — a picnic lunch, delicious
layers of color, fresh water blue, orange
granite, cream sand, chocolate earth, wild
green berry bushes, deep salt water blue
beneath white frosting clouds in a cool blue
mint sky — thin strips lying naturally
on top of each other —

• • •

hours later, near the end of our stroll
along our meandering, self guided trail,
approaching sunset, on a shaded point,
alone on the rim of the quarry, inhaling
deeply the darker colors, the quiet,
the holy time,

watching the only other life —
two white seagulls taking their evening
freshwater bath in the quarry blue, playing,
fluttering their wings, washing off
the salt and sand of another day,

while above the whole scene, a long thin cloud —
an elongated giant, a ghostly human form,
right arm outstretched in an Australian crawl,
swims steadily, surely across the horizon,
through glittering tongues of flame.

Sunset in a Strong Wind

The clouds won't stay still. Just
when I think I see something, just when
it all makes sense, when the orange heads
glowing above our dark cloaks provide
sudden illumination, the cloaks are torn
into tatters, whipped away, leaving only
bright stripes and dark bars which bend, break
dissolve in the pouring wind, the wind
an invisible broom sweeping all the unused
grey-pink particles into that dark grey,
rapidly turning black
thickening mass on the far horizon,

into ye olde cosmic dustbin —

the remains — three small peach croissants
with a small cup of dark coffee —
for tomorrow's breakfast.

That will have to do.

Stretching to Infinity

I

peaceful harbor waters, alternating currents,
light and dark grey layers mirroring
the clouds and sky, the light grey ripples
turning pinker in the reflection of the reflection
of the setting sun — the dark grey
getting darker, but not as dark
as the black finger rock island

peaceful safe harbor waters
with birds, buoys, and boats, all afloat,
drifting across my rippling lines.

II

moments later, on the rock wall
collar of Bearskin Neck, looking back
at our point of origin, at Front Beach,
at the harbor ablaze with the direct rays
of sunset —
                                        innumerable tongues
of red fire getting darker every time
I look up from the page —
                                                                I am struck
by the process, the sun going down,
the streetlights on the road behind
the beach going on, their long yellow lines
cutting across the barely glowing coals,

III

finally, the two human heads —
in the water, dark corks, afloat,
bobbing, moving ever so slowly further
and further away,

crossing the bars of light,
swimming together in the night sea.

The Mirror

On the love seat, lying on my left side,
head resting on your right shoulder,

looking dreamily

into the full length antique mirror
on our living room wall, halfway between
the door and the picture window,

looking at the image of itself with you
under the large print of Monet's water lilies
drifting under the bridge . . .

at the image

in the glass within the deep cherry frame,
within the mirror, the sanded, redone mirror
saturated with tung oil, reclaimed from the house,
the old dump in West Boylston,

the head thinking
of a ten-year-old boy thinking, really thinking
of death, understanding for the first time
that one day he will be no more, the boy
awake at three in the morning, standing
alone in the narrow darkened hallway
in front of this same mirror, staring
shaking, staring, shaking some more,

staring at his unique configuration of atoms
for what seemed a lifetime until finally
the shaking stopped and he came to himself . . .

the head resting, looking at its glasses
in the mirror, the glasses transformed into shades,
into forest green discs reflecting the leaves
of the tree outside and the shifting amoeba
blots of pale blue —
two eyes of sky
shining through, glowing holes, tunnels
through time, through the center of the head
to the land of the dead.

The Unthinking Rhythm of the Sea

For Alice LePoer Scrimgeour (March 8, 1909 - January 14, 1981)

I

Sitting there
in the old maple chair
                                        for years
your grossly overweight body
                                        permanently
misshaping the dirt-encrusted cushions,

wearing the one tattered filthy dress
day in and day out
                                        for years
the tip of your stubby right forefinger
aimlessly swirling whirls and whirls —
circles of salt (that couldn't keep you
from looking back)

moving round and around and over the old
oak table's ingrained dirt brown surface —

tip, grains, and table worn smooth

moving in the same endless
unthinking rhythm as the sea . . .

your fingers moving in that same rhythm —
stacking and unstacking red, white, and blue
children's blocks (American Bricks,
the ancestor of LEGO) building and tearing down
your own simple houses, simple structures
you could live in — subconscious structures —
better than *Better Homes* designs,

and sometimes at the old piano
in the living room — your fingers
still moving in rhythm, sliding round
and around and over the black and white,
the sharps and flats, playing over and over again
your own composition, your one song
                                                            until
the keys — one by one — went out
like lights before bedtime . . .

and with that old beat up scrabble set,
sliding the square box shaped wooden letters

into word after random word — long words
sprawled all over the board,
                                        trying to play
all the letters — no interest in points
or high scores — each word valuable
for its own sake.
                                        Ah! words, words,
some words you wouldn't use
                                        (neither in games
nor in real life) some words like "cat"
had bad connotations — better to use
"feline quadruped" you said . . .

sitting there in that chair
looking out the living room window
                    looking past the overgrown
baseball field, looking at
the oak tree in which your elder son
once nailed together a tree house,
a tree house with electricity (lights
and radio) his refuge and fortress —

also, it appears, an eyesore
torn down one night by neighbors . . .

sitting, telling your son of
                                        your lone vote
in the mock high school election —
the only Democrat in a school of Republicans —

the principal's anger, his interrogation,
"Why? Why? I know your father's a Republican."

"Yes, but my mother is a Democrat," you replied,

and telling that same son about clippings
of toenails and fingernails — explaining
that one's nails are unique
                                        and, therefore,
must be destroyed,
                                        they might turn up
at the scene of a crime — be used
as evidence against you, you said . . .

sitting, thinking perhaps of more, more
than the sturdy oak, the kind gentle husband
and the four randomly sprouting children —

thinking perhaps of your mother's letter
preserved on the bottom of the bottom drawer,
apologizing

for not having the money to attend
your college graduation, the letter
simply stating

how tired she was of housework
and expressing

her dream: " . . . perhaps you could do
some of the things I dreamed of
but never did . . ."

thinking perhaps of yourself, your Colby education,
your honors in history, thinking perhaps

of your dreams of being
a teacher, a lawyer, an architect,
an author of mysteries . . .

Ah! . . . dreams . . . dreams . . . dreams . . .

II

dreams . . . white wisps of dissolving cloud
swirling across blue sky —
myself dreaming . . .

thinking of
you with my father on one
of your long walks by the reservoir . . .

Ah! . . . the pines . . . the bright blue
future sky . . . the soft bed of needles . . .
the water (kind and gentle) lapping
at the shore . . .

and, consequently, you pulling me,
your toddler son through the depression,
through the house without electricity,
through the corn meal mush for breakfast,
lunch, supper, and breakfast again — cheaper,
better for you than oatmeal, you said . . .

of my telling you of one day
in my 2nd grade classroom

discussing housecleaning —
how everyone does it differently —

"My mother,"
I steadfastly maintained, "just sweeps
the dirt into corners and leaves it there."

The teacher — confused, trying to help,
"She must pick it up later — sometime."

No, I stubbornly, insisted,
"She just leaves it there."...

of your visits to school, observing,
sitting in the back of the class, the teacher
perturbed, the class giggling, pointing,
"Is that your mother," they whispered ...

thinking of once, the surprise visit
of your college friend and field hockey teammate,
your friend — transformed into a celebrity,
a talent scout in my ten year old mind —

me singing
"Rudolph, the Red-Nosed Reindeer" over and over,
round and around and over the adult conversation,

"Doesn't he know any other songs?" she asked
shortly before leaving — never to return ...

of when I was thirteen — your washing
my stained sheets, and watching one morning
before breakfast — me squirming under the blankets
of my bed (the couch in the living room)
no blame (nor praise)
just "I know
what you're doing!"

years later, myself — still thinking
"knowledge is power," ...

still thinking of your anger
after one of the rare visits
of your husband's elder brother, after
the visit of Uncle Karl and Aunt Ella
(his older cousin/wife) Aunt Ella standing
all the while, wearing her mink coat
in the old dump, sharing her knowledge

of how to roll one sock into a ball
inside the other to keep the pair intact

"If there's one thing I don't need, it's
housekeeping hints from that woman,"
and later
"Their kids are adopted," you said,

myself still thinking of their gleaming new
Cadillac — so out of place — parked
in our narrow rutted dirt driveway . . .

and thinking about Sundays, our scrubbed
faces, clean clothes, the long walk
down the steep hill to the bus stop
and the hour long ride to the Christian
Science Church (and Sunday School) until
I was old enough to understand what
they were saying about disease and death
being only in the mind.
"We only want
you to go until you are old enough
to decide for yourself," you said.

"I'm old enough now." I replied
and you let it lie . . .

and one of the last times, outside
you and me in the bright sun,
standing just off first base
in the center of what once was
a cluster of berry bushes, discussing
free love and marriage.
Ah! but . . .
"The children! Somebody's got to
take care of the children," you said.

III

There, in the chair — alone
for the last
five years after your husband died,

the extra weight withering away —
leaving you
with neither strength nor will to stop
those neighborhood teenage girls from
walking through
your unlocked doors — those girls laughing,
taunting you, blowing marijuana smoke
in your face, stealing what little you had left . . .

there, in the chair,
still tracing circles of salt (lace designs
beside the cooling untouched meals on wheels)

your glazed eyes and monotone
reveal you are far away:

*"When we were married — October 10,
1936, we sat in the living room of my
father's house, the house we lived in
when you were born, the house
that just burned down,*

*"The fire was low in the fireplace.
We sat on a lumpy brown settee, as
the Reverend Brady asked us: 'Do you
promise to love honor and cherish,'*
***I would not say obey**, 'for the rest
of your life, til death do you part?'*

*"My father and mother and brother
were among the guests.
Your Uncle Karl
did not attend."*

Mom! Ah, mom! Some things
you couldn't let lie . . .

Words, words! Your words, mine, cloud wisps
whispers that won't be still,

won't allow easy closure,
won't let me end with you sitting
in that encrusted chair,
the matted grey hair
piled on your head, looking out the window,
with you
just sitting in that chair
with the other
decaying things in the old dump
we had to pry you out of near the end . . .

won't simply let me end with death, the death
of Alice LePoer Scrimgeour, — Hahnemann Hospital,
Worcester, Massachusetts, January 14, 1981.

("She died as she lived," the Doctor said,
"without the aid of doctors.")

At the nurses' station, I learn
there's been "a slight mistake," that
you're "still alive, but not for long."

In the room, I look at the tubes,
at your frail frame, listen to you breathe —
so faint — yet easy
and take your hand
in both of mine —
(as I couldn't do
this afternoon, when I pried your desperate hands
away from that dirty old headboard because I
could not leave you to die in <u>that</u> house you had
not stepped outside of in over twenty years — without
giving you one last chance, without turning you over
to the despised doctors and bringing you to the hospital —
the last resort)
our hands fused
into a cable, a cord that holds us
close for half an hour — a cord

that snapped in two
when you withdrew,

leaving a high voltage power line dangling —
sparkling, lashing — random writhing in the wind . . .

Nor with the service, the do-good minister
(we never saw before or since) mouthing
my brother's prompt, the too easy,

"She was born too soon —
years before her time." . . .

We all are what we are; I am your son
sitting at my computer in my own house,
tapping all too random keys, watching
these words, these white wisps of cloud
swirl round and around and over
the smooth blue sky surface,
white wisps
in invisible, everflowing currents,
glimpses in passing —
of the inexorable, unfathomable, grinding process —
of human beings caught in that same
endless,
unthinking rhythm as the sea.

Rocking with Quinn

at 6:30 am — everyone else, my wife,
my daughter, her husband, resting after
the creation, after the first six days

of my grandson's life, rocking
in the chair we bought as a baby
present, rocking in the same basic,

elemental rhythm as the sea, the strands
of grey beard on my bowed chin mingling
with Quinn's wispy newborn locks —

the slight shudder that shakes
his entire body — goes through
me also — the warmth of his small

6 day old head seeps through his new
outfit, his blanket, my rainbow trout
T shirt to my chest, just as

my warmth seeps through to him —
so peaceful, so quiet, so serene,
as the swaddling cloth, our clothes,

the newborn and aging skin dissolve
in the stream of spirit traveling
both ways — like the warmth

mingling together — as if we were
not already, would not always be
merged, as if any combination of cloth

and flesh could ever keep us apart.

Acknowledgments

Heartfelt appreciation to: John Briggs, Leo Connellan, J. W. Rivers, Christine Xanthakos Scrimgeour, Xanthi Scrimgeour, Robert D. Sutherland, and Bill Tremblay.

Special thanks to the Connecticut State University System for the research grants which enabled me to write many of these poems and to J. D. Scrimgeour and Jamie Scrimgeour for their many contributions to this manuscript.

The Faces, *Poetry Digest*, Winter 1996.
Judge Corwin's Bedroom, *The Galley Sail Review*, forthcoming.
Lines Started Outside Filene's Basement . . . , *Rio Grande Review*, Fall 1991.
War Game, *We Speak for Peace*, (anthology) 1993, *Hobo Jungle*, Spring 1989.
This Morning, *Hammers*, 1992.
Challenger, *Live Poets*, (anthology) Islip, NY, 1992, *Poems that Thump in the Dark*, 1995.
Ant, *Register Citizen*, July 31, 1994.
Human Brain: Figure 11.1, *The Cape Rock*, 1992.
(from) Mohegan Bluffs, "The Sinister Seemingly Playful," and "With My Back to the Sea," *The Works*, September 1993.
Salt Marsh, *KARAMU*, Spring 1995.
Terns Nesting Area: Do not Disturb, *KARAMU*, Spring 1995.
Crow Lake, *Green Mountains Review*, November 1995.
In the Fog, *PenWorks*, Spring 1993.
Who's Blind Round This House Anyway, *Dikel Your Hands*, Spoon River Press, 1979, *Bird in the Heart*, (anthology) forthcoming.
Breaking the Bread, *Harp Strings*, August 1993.
A Miracle, *Byline*, April 1996.
On the Lawn of Our Lady, *Poetry Digest*, Winter 1996.
Just Returning, *Fingerlings*, (anthology) Catamount Press, Spring 1995.
The French Impressionist Idea, *Green Mountains Review*, Summer/Fall 1993.
Babson Farm Quarry, *Illinois Review*, Fall 1995.
Sunset in a Strong Wind, *Hobo Jungle*, Autumn 1990.

Cover design: Demetri Kasperson & Jamie Scrimgeour

James R. Scrimgeour received his BA from Clark University and his MA and PhD from the University of Massachusetts, Amherst. Since 1968, he has taught a wide variety of literature and writing courses at a number of colleges and universities — including the last 17 years at Western Connecticut State University where he served as Department Chair from 1983-1987 and as Coordinator of Graduate Studies in English from 1987 to the present. He has, for the past 10 years, been associated with *Connecticut Review* — first as Associate Editor (1987-1993) then as Editor (1993-1996) and finally as Editor Emeritus (1996-present). Furthermore, he has edited a bicentennial anthology of American poetry and published a critical biography of Sean O'Casey (G.K. Hall), a book of original poems (*Dikel, Your Hands*, Spoon River Poetry Press), numerous articles and reviews on various aspects of poetry and drama, and over 150 poems in small press magazines and anthologies. He and his wife, Christine Xanthakos Scrimgeour, currently reside in New Milford, CT and will celebrate their 33rd wedding anniversary on October 13, 1996.

The PIKESTAFF PRESS